CDH Stars and Angels

Congenital Diaphragmatic Hernia Awareness

Issue 1: January 2018

Brenda M. Mertes

ISBN:1983544523
ISBN-13:9781983544521

<u>On This Page</u>

A Word From The Author

My own son was diagnosed with Congenital Diaphragmatic Hernia in 2015. This is when a baby's diaphragm fails to completely form at teen weeks into a mother's pregnancy. Congenital Diaphragmatic Hernia isn't "just a hernia". It takes the lives of babies and can even take the lives of older survivors at any point in their lives. Any parent who has gone through this with their child knows how important it is to raise awareness and funds for research for these babies. Doctors all over the world work tirelessly to find a reason that Congenital Diaphragmatic Hernia occurs in babies and if it can be prevented.

Other ways that can help parents that are dealing with this birth defect, is by keeping your sick kids at home. One fact about CDH is that the immune systems of these babies are very fragile and while they may survive the repair surgery and their stay in the neonatal intensive care unit, survivors can die from respiratory infections. Common places that people have brought their sick kids include church nurseries and schools. I hope that by raising awareness for this condition, the public will be more considerate when deciding if it's more important to bring their sick kid to school and possibly end the life of someone else, or keep them safely home.

This isn't a diagnosis that almost everyone has heard of. Upon hearing of my own son's diagnosis of CDH, I couldn't wrap my head around whether this was a death sentence for him or not. My anatomy scan where I learned that I was having the boy that I always wanted, turned into a horrific day for me. This isn't a story that is far from the experience that other parents of babies with this diagnosis have.

Furthermore, parents with babies diagnosed with this birth defect deal with a lot of emotional damage after watching our babies fight for their lives. It is difficult to sit beside our child's hospital bed and not be able to touch or hold them while he/she is being constantly poked and prodded with tubes and needles. It's not easy wondering if our babies will make it out of surgery and what their recovery will be like. The fear that the hole in our child's diaphragm might reopen is always in the back of our minds. The likelihood of that happening (called reherniation) is something that we have to constantly consider. Therefore, it is common for parents to suffer from Post Traumatic Stress Disorder and similar problems long after their CDH survivor is grown.

Ever since my son had his repair surgery, I built an online group for parents of these babies and older survivors themselves, to communicate to each other and support one another. Through this, parents have learned what questions they should ask their doctors, found other members with similar stories to theirs, and commemorated the babies who have gained their wings. This magazine features the stories of some of those parents who were willing to share, and the photographs of survivors that we call our "CDH Stars". My hopes for this magazine – and in sharing the stories of these parents and the survivors – is that more of the world will learn about this birth defect and what efforts are necessary to help possibly prevent future occurrences.

– Brenda M. Mertes

<u>Lily Atkinson – CDH Star and Fighter</u>

Our CDH Story did not follow the usual pattern. I had a straight-forward pregnancy, no concerns with any scans or tests throughout. Until, that is, I went for a routine growth scan at 36 weeks. Then our world was turned upside down. The sonographer went really quiet, left the room, and when she returned she had a senior doctor with her. The two of them looked at my ultrasound again and then they said, "Your baby's stomach is where her lung should be. It's not good".

When I asked the obvious, "Is my baby going to die?" I was told to prepare for the worst. I was referred onto a specialist hospital that same day and we got a glimmer of hope back. We learned the term Congenital Diaphragmatic Hernia. We were told the baby had a 50/50 survival rate. Still not great odds but better than nothing!

Because I was diagnosed so late on in my pregnancy, the next three weeks were a whirlwind of scans, appointments, injections, MRIs, tours of NICU, meetings with consultants, specialists, and midwives. I found CDH UK at this point and joined the Facebook support group, where I found other families going through the same roller coaster of emotions as I was.

Despite being told not to "Google" it, my curiosity got the better of me and of course I found some horror stories. The sad truth is that with a 50/50 survival rate, for every positive outcome there is a story that doesn't end so happily. I tried to stay positive but I struggled every day. I take my hat off to all the families that find out about CDH early in their pregnancies. I only knew for a few weeks and it felt like eternity!

I was booked in to be induced when I was 39 weeks and 2 days pregnant, at the Southern General Hospital in Glasgow. The plan was to try for a natural birth to stimulate lung function. The baby would then be incubated and paralysed straight away and be moved to Yorkhill Hospital when she was stable. After a few days, and some issues with her heart rate dropping, it became clear that our daughter was a stubborn one and Lily was born by emergency C-section on the 18th February 2015.

She was immediately incubated and taken to the NICU. We didn't get to see her until 6 hours later. She was stabilised fairly quickly and moved to Yorkhill Hospital the next day. Having been through major surgery myself, I wasn't ready to be discharged. So for a few days, Lily and I were in two different hospitals and my husband had to go backwards and forwards between the two. Very quickly I was back on my feet and discharge and got to see Lily in the NICU. The doctors were surprised by how stable she had been from birth and began to mention that she was a candidate for laparascopic (keyhole) repair surgery.

They stressed that she would have to tick certain boxes for this to happen so we tried not to get our hopes up. Keyhole repair surgery is still relatively new and the surgeons were clear that if they felt as if it were too much for Lily, as it is a lengthier procedure, they would revert to the standard method. Her stats remained stable and they decided to proceed with keyhole repair surgery on the 6th day of her life.

Lily was in theatre for 6 hours. Although I could have sworn that it was closer to a week, as time seemed to go backwards at some point!! When we saw the lead surgeon return he told us the surgery had been a success, that the laparascopic method had worked and that the hernia had been small and had been repaired using only 5 stitches. We have never been so relieved, another step closer to home! From that moment on, Lily went from strength to strength, She established feeding quickly after she decided to pull her NG tube out, successfully weaned off her medication and was able to move into the high dependency unit where I was able to stay with her round the clock. We were home 2 weeks and 6 days after her birth.

Lily has had very few complications since her repair surgery. Her left lung is growing slowly and is now up to around 50% of the size it should be. Her consultant has said that, all being well, we expect it to be around 90% size by the time she's 2 years old.

We've been incredibly lucky but it's still early days for us. To the untrained eye Lily looks like any other baby, which leads to complacency when in truth CDH will always be a huge factor in Lily's life, and in ours.

-Kimberly Atkinson

<u>The Journey To Grace – Journal Entry</u>

Bobby Evans of Fort Worth, Texas wrote a journal to cope with his emotions during the trying times that his daughter was in the NICU fighting for her life. Below is his entry – word for word – bringing to awareness not only the struggles of Congenital Diaphragmatic Hernia itself, but the thoughts and feelings that run deep for parents while helplessly watching their babies fight.

<u>By Bobby Evans</u>

How it all began:

My story starts the day I took my first step on my journey to Grace. It was December 24th, 2012, Christmas Eve. I had worked half a day and had a list of things that needed to get done after work to get ready for a family dinner on Christmas Day. My wife hadn't been herself in over a month; she was ill around Thanksgiving and hadn't popped back from it. She was constantly tired, weak and generally didn't feel like doing much. We had been to her doctor, and were told she had allergies. We tried the medicine he prescribed and no changes happened, so a week or two later we went back. Allergies again, this time she got a steroid shot! We left with the hopes that all would be well soon but it wasn't. This went on and I was getting concerned for her health but at the same time frustrated on the inside because she didn't want to do anything, and she tried, but I could tell that whenever we did leave to go do something that she didn't feel well. That Christmas Eve, when I got home and started to get things together so we could go get what we needed, she didn't feel like going. I had had it, I said, come on, we are going to the hospital! She disagreed because she is stubborn and after twenty minutes of explaining to her that we needed to figure out what was going on because this isn't normal, she reluctantly agreed! I think she only agreed to go because she was tired of feeling that way, not that she agreed with me.

We told our two children, 18 and 10 at the time that we were going to the hospital just to get mommy checked and that we would be back in a little while, and we left. We went to our local emergency room and checked in at the front desk, filled out the paperwork and sat down. It was a relatively calm evening, just a few people in there, not much going on. After a few minutes the reception nurse called my wife's name and handed her a cup and instructed her to please see if she could urinate in the cup while we were waiting. My wife obliged and sat back down next to me and put her head on my shoulder. Twenty minutes passed and then they called us into the triage room. The nurse was polite, asked what my wife's symptoms were and began taking her blood pressure and temperature. All came back normal, so they directed us to the back into private rooms to await a doctor. Another twenty minutes passed and as we sat in the quiet room alone, silently concerned that something major was wrong with my wife, I tried to crack jokes to make her smile! I hit on a couple, bombed on a few and just as I think she was about to tell me to just be quiet, the doctor walked in. He had a nurse with him, and clipboard in hand and looking down at the clipboard, without even really making eye contact began to speak the words that would forever change my life.

"Mrs. Evans, the symptoms you have described to us are most likely caused by your pregnancy, were you unaware that you are pregnant?"

See those words; those amazing words had to take a minute to register in my caveman brain. See that wasn't possible, we have been trying for 10 years to get pregnant with no success. I knew the problem was with me and she disagreed with me, but it had to be, she had 2 children prior to me. These two children are my children in every aspect except biology.

None the less, she obviously could get pregnant so the problem had to be with me. We got some preliminary testing done, and everything looked normal on my end but to really tell, I had to do some extensive, expensive testing that my insurance would not cover and we aren't exactly rolling in the dough so to speak. have a mediocre job that I've been at for almost 12 years, I make decent money and she has worked sporadically here and there but I've always liked it better when she didn't work, when she was there to always handle anything that needed to be done with the kids. We made it work, but we really couldn't handle any surprises or expensive tests like the ones required to undoubtedly tell if something was wrong with my reproductive system or not. Needless to say, when the doctor kind of matter of factly spoke those words, I couldn't believe them. Maria and I looked at each other and mentally asked ourselves, "did he just say what I think he said?" After I was able to catch my breath and the blood had flowed back into my brain and all cognitive functions had resumed, the doctor began to go over all the common sense things to do and not do, and then he told us we would need to find an OBGYN to get further analysis but that they were going to do a routine sonogram to determine how pregnant we were.

We went to the room and the nurse had my wife undress and put on the elegant hospital gown. She then layed her down on the examining table and got the machine they use for the procedure and she began looking at a screen. I looked as well and it looked like a game of space invaders, I just saw black and grey, nothing stood out and then the nurse said there you go, there is your baby. I saw a grey circle, didn't look like much but it was somewhat moving, and the nurse took some measurements and said that we were approximately 8 weeks pregnant. Maria and I looked at each other, then looked at our little grey circle in amazement. We were ecstatic. While at the hospital, I called my mother in law to relay the news, and my wife could hear her scream with joy over the phone. My mother and father in law showed up at the hospital in about minutes and came to see us and congratulate us. The doctors discharged us with a lot of paperwork and instructed us to follow up with an Obgyn in a few days after the holidays. We went home on cloud 9, we couldn't have asked for a better Christmas.

<u>Reality Sets In</u>

We talked about how we would tell the kids. I was happy but all of a sudden got a little scared. See our children were technically my step children. I had raised them both to be my own however, and in my eyes they were. My son was now a young man, 18 years old at that time and I knew it would be no big deal to him but our daughter, who so skillfully had me wrapped around her little finger from the moment I saw her, whom I had helped raise since she was 5 days old, how would she take it. I knew in my heart that there would be no difference between any of the kids in my eyes, they were all my children and would all be treated the same, but how does a 10 year old understand that. How can I show her that I love her just as much as I always have and that just because this new little sibling was coming along that she wouldn't feel different and that my love for her wouldn't skip a beat. Maria began to help me see straight as she always does, Malformation. He then began to explain it to us that when the baby's lungs are developing, sometimes this forms and it takes up space, or shifts the heart from where it is supposed to be. It is a serious condition but it can be handled and we just had to monitor it on a weekly basis to make sure that fluid, or Hydrops didn't develop and cause more issues. We were scared and I began searching on the internet immediately, I read everything I could about the condition and talked to my wife about it. I felt confident enough that we were in good hands and that we could beat this without a hitch. We had ups and downs emotionally but there are many things out there worse than a CCAM and we were going to beat this.

<u>The roller coaster ride continues</u>

With this issue, we had to get a sonogram on a weekly basis. The baby had to be monitored closely to make sure that the fluid, known as Hydrops didn't start to build up and cause problems. The weeks came and went, and the baby grew, there was no evidence of hydrops and we began feeling more confident. The doctors instructed us that with this issue, we would need to deliver in a hospital with a specialized NICU unit rather than our local hospital. This was a little bit upsetting but our choices were 30 miles in either direction to Austin, or San Antonio. We talked about it and decided we would go with San Antonio because our local obgyn, whom we had still been seeing for routine tests had a friend there who was a doctor so we felt like it would all move smoother. We toured the hospital and were quite impressed, we registered there to deliver our baby, and her due date was August 4th, 2013. We notched another task off of our belt and continued on with our local and Austin appointments.

Things were going well and my wife was starting to show now. It kind of jumped; she went from not showing at all to having a significant baby bump. We began shopping for maternity clothes for her and baby clothes for our new daughter. It was fun. We had thought up some names prior to knowing the sex, and once we found out, we had the name chosen. Mariah, derived from my wife's beloved grandmother's first name and middle initial. It was perfect, but now I was tasked with picking out a middle name. It was hard for me, I had no idea where to start, and not to say it wasn't important to me, but I procrastinated for quite a bit on it, to the point where Maria would get mad, she thought I didn't care, which wasn't the case, I guess I was just scared. I was still in shock that we were having a baby.

All the realities really sank into my head about the finances, and we have a 3 bedroom house and all bedrooms are used, so what would we do in the future. I wasted a lot of time thinking about preparing, rather than sitting down and drinking in the water so to speak. One thing I did learn, its all going to happen, and happen when its ready whether you are prepared or not, but you know what.. It's all going to be ok, because we are a family, we are together and we take on everything as a family. Once I set that into my rock hard head, I started thinking of names. I said many over and over in my mind, I was listening for rhythmic meshing, I didn't want anything that she could get made fun of in school, you know the typical parent worries, and what not. I came across one that as soon as I said it, I felt something.

It was Grace, Mariah Grace Evans. I liked the sound of that. So that was her name from that point on. It was towards the end of April now and our weekly viewings into Mariah's world were going well, Maria was big, and Mariah was measuring big too. They noticed a little bit of fluid building up in Mariah's abdomen and we just needed to watch it closely to make sure it doesn't increase. The doctors also started scratching their heads a little bit on this visit. They wouldn't quite tell us what was going on but I could see concern in his eyes, and when he began consulting one of the other physicians I asked what was going on. He stated that he wasn't quite sure but the malformation wasn't acting like a CCAM does, he said that now the issue looks quite different than it did last week. After a few minutes of going back and forth the doctor said that what they thought was a CCAM now appears to be a CDH (Congenital Diaphragmatic Hernia) and that this is a whole new ballpark. They explained to us what it was, that when the baby is developing, somewhere around the 8-10th week of development, when the diaphragm is forming, something didn't form right and there is a hole in the diaphragm.

This causes the internal organs below the diaphragm to migrate up into the chest cavity. Depending on the size of the hole, and how much of what organs are up in the chest determine the severity. It was too soon to tell in our case but since it was enough to push her heart all the way over to the left side chest cavity, they were pretty sure it was significant and that this is a major issue now. They advised us that we needed to get an Amniocentesis test along with some other optional genetic testing to determine if there were any other factors that sometimes come along with this defect. We agreed to the testing. We freaked out again, and now everything I had learned over the last few weeks about CCAM's meant nothing because this is an entirely different issue. I once again began combing the internet and this time, the things I found were not so positive. I learned that only 50% of children diagnosed with CDH survive.

I learned that along with CDH many other problems can occur. Babies with CDH often have trouble drinking milk, and have problems regurgitating. Hearing loss is connected to CDH somehow. Depending on the size of the hole in the diaphragm, if its too big, it will have to be patched with a gore-tex patch, and in that case, the patch doesn't grow with the child, so later on in life, there are high probabilities that the muscle will tear away from the patch and the hernia will re-appear requiring another surgery. Depending on how much the lungs have been inhibited, it can cause life long problems with breathing, chronic asthma and many other issues.

It was at this point that I really wished it was a CCAM instead of this. The results came back from the Amniocentesis test and everything was normal, we then opted for further genetic testing and everything came back normal as well there. They look for genes that point to Down syndrome, Trisome 13 and 18 and a few other indicators but we came back all normal. We left the doctor's office unsure of what we had just been through, unable to understand all that had just been told to us and scared to death of what was in the future. We were told to continue our weekly visits there in Austin, and to continue our routine checkups with our OBGYN in San Marcos, so we did.

The doctors had great communication between themselves and our local OBGYN was aware of our situation, we went in for a visit and she talked with us. We asked for her opinion on this, and she is a realist, she told us that in her 20 yr carrier, that she had seen 5 babies with this issue, and had never seen one come home. Our hearts sank, and I tried to keep it together for my wife's sake and my own, but inside my heart was pounding, I was questioning my faith, why had this happened to us, why after trying so long, to the point where we accepted the fact that we couldn't have a baby, and that the love of my 2 other children was enough, would we be blessed with a baby, and then have something so horrible go wrong. I couldn't wrap my head around it but I had to stay calm. She also began to talk to us about the treatment issues, that if we decided to treat, that some of the procedures could damage Maria where she couldn't get pregnant again, and that we needed to weigh the pros and cons if we wanted to go all out and try to save a baby that potentially wouldn't make it, or if we wanted to start over.

This wasn't even an issue with us, we didn't have to discuss it with each other for a second, we were going to do whatever was humanly possible to have little Mariah Grace running around our feet. Needless to say, we left the doctors office that day feeling quite hollow and lost. We had another appointment in Austin later that week and when we showed up they did the usual sonogram and they noticed that one, my wife was huge for being around 6 months pregnant, and 2, the fluid in the baby's abdomen had started to increase. I had noticed my wife getting larger, but remember this is the first time I have ever been the 2nd party to a pregnancy, I had only seen pregnant woman out and about and I don't know how big you are supposed to be at what point in the pregnancy. My wife had become quite uncomfortable in the last week or so, she was short of breath and couldn't walk 50 feet without having to rest. The doctors noted that and said that we might need to perform an amniotic reduction. After reviewing what they saw the doctor asked us if we would consider flying to Boston, , to a specialist that could see us. We immediately said yes, without thinking of how we would handle all of this, and the doctor said he would call and see what he could set up. We went home, again, upset and not knowing what we were going to do.

<u>We got our hope back</u>

Later that day we got a call from the doctor in Austin, unfortunately the hospital in Boston wouldn't be able to see us for about 6 weeks and the doctors didn't feel we had that much time. He then said that they referred him to the Texas

Children's Hospital located in Houston, Texas about 3 and an half hours from us. They called them and gave them our info and they set us up an appointment to see if we were qualified to become patients there. Our appointment was set, they called us with an itinerary and it was set for May 9th. This just so happens to be the day after our anniversary so we spent the evening of our anniversary driving to Houston to get ready for the appointment. It was okay because at that time, all either one of us could think about was what was going on with our baby. We did stop and have a dinner at a nice restaurant which somewhat lightened the mood. We made it to the hotel and got settled in to go to our appointment the next morning. On that morning we arrived at TCH and right away I was taken back.

The place is huge. Luckily we had an itinerary that told us exactly where to show up and when we did, they checked us in and gave my wife a folder and told us to sit in the lobby and we would be called shortly. After a few minutes a nurse walked out and called my wife's name, we stood up and followed her down a hallway; she began small talk with us and directed us to an examination room. Once inside, she directed my wife to an exam bed to lie on and began prepping for a sonogram. She began the sonogram and there was a screen right in front of me to watch, at this point I really didn't like watching the sonograms because I was paranoid, and any little thing I saw was a concern so a lot of the time, I stared down at my shoes. She did all the routine checks and measurements and took some notes.

When she was done, she said that she was going to let the doctor know and the doctor would come in to talk to us. We waited a few minutes and the doctor came in. She introduced herself and then asked if it was ok if she reexamined my wife. She looked at a few things and then told us that from what she saw, it looked like a right sided hernia, and that most commonly they are on the left hand side, she also said that it appears to be her liver that is up inside her chest cavity and that they needed to do a fetal MRI and also wanted to do a EKG to get some baseline numbers. We agreed and went on to the MRI appointment. I wasn't allowed to go into the MRI with my wife because as a child I was shot in the leg with a BB gun and the BB was still in there, and apparently the MRI machine could cause problems with it, so I sat outside and waited, for about an hour. When that was done, we went to the EKG which was just like a sonogram but they just monitored the heart.

When all this was done we were exhausted, it had taken up the whole day, we had one appointment left. It was a consultation with another doctor. They directed us to a small waiting room and had us wait, my wife was exhausted and I wasn't too energetic myself. After what seemed like an hour, but was probably more like 20 minutes, a knock on the door was heard and in walked a doctor. He introduced himself as Dr. Cass and he proceeded to tell us that he would be the doctor performing the hernia repair surgery after our daughter is born. He told us that he has been doing this for many years and has developed a spectrum of things to look for that will tell him somewhat how a baby will do once born and how much intervention they would need. He told us that all the tests on our baby showed that she was in very good shape to handle what was ahead, and that it appeared that her liver was encased in a rare membrane sac that has kept the issue from becoming much worse, He said it appeared that 46% of her liver was up in her chest which was quite a bit but it *didn't appear to be too much of an issue. They measured something called head to lung ratio and it was on the better side of the spectrum so he was very optimistic that we would come out just fine. He told us he wanted to see us in about a month and to continue with our weekly appointments in Austin. We set up our appointment for June 10th and drove back to San Marcos.*

We continued with our weekly appointments in Austin and had quit seeing our local OBGYN because at this point there was nothing really that she could do. Maria was huge at this point, and during the sonogram measurements Mariah was approaching the 7lb area and she wasn't due until August. They told us that it was due to the fluid in her abdomen making her abdomen large which was messing with the calculations, they also noted how uncomfortable my wife was and asked us when our next appointment was in Houston. We told them June 10th, and they said that they were going to call and see if they could see us sooner because my wife had too much amniotic fluid around the baby and it could trick her into early labor. We went home and waited to hear from the doctors. We got a phone call a few days later and it was TCH saying that they could get us in for June 6th instead of June 10th if we would like. So my wife called and asked me if that was ok since I had to take off of work. I arranged it and we went.

<u>Mariah the magnificent</u>

When we found out that our baby had CDH, as I mentioned it before, I studied it on the internet to no end. I had read countless cases and knew what the doctors were looking for and what to expect. After Mariah got stable, they began watching her oxygenation percentages. She started out around an 86% oxygen level. You and I breathe an oxygen level around 21%. This is what's known as room air in the medical world, and that is where she needed to be. They also took x-rays to determine what shape her lungs were in and to determine how soon they would perform the surgery to repair the hernia. Originally we were told they would do the surgery about a week later, but when she was 3 days old they decided to go ahead and do it. It was a hectic time for us. The day they wanted to do the surgery, our daughter was going to be on her way back from Dallas with her biological father.

He was supposed to deliver her to us but as usual, the plans changed and he was unable to make that happen. Maria wanted her back, so did I for that matter but I did not want to be on the road when they were doing the surgery, I wanted to be there at the hospital. I had Maria contact him and the night prior to the surgery, I drove halfway to meet them and pick her up. I was already tired, and by the time I got back with Celeste it was around 2am. I didn't care; I picked up my baby and now was nervously waiting for surgery for our other baby. The surgery was supposed to start around 1pm but it got postponed until about 3.

They performed the surgery right in the room that Mariah was in, they sterilized the whole room and didn't let anyone in that didn't have anything to do with the surgery. We stayed in Maria's hospital room and anxiously waited the phone call. About 5pm we received the phone call. The surgery was a success. They were able to pull her liver down from her chest and move it to where it was supposed to be. The hole in her diaphragm was too large to stitch itself up so they had to put a patch in. I was hoping that they didn't have to do that because in my research, the patches often have to be re-sewn later on in life because they do not grow with the muscle. Apparently it isn't too difficult or major of a surgery but none the less, I would rather not have to have that happen. Immediately after the surgery, they took an x-ray and the doctors were quite astounded. Mariah's heart had moved almost completely over to where it was supposed to be situated and her lungs showed significantly more area then they had originally perceived. This was great news to us. She was just through the first major hurdle and had passed with flying colors. She had a small bandage on her tummy where the incision was and over the next few days all she did was sleep because she was on a morphine drip. We would go sit and watch her sleep, she was so beautiful.

Maria began reading her a children's bible that my sister had sent us. It was an everyday ritual. I would wheel her down there and she would read from the bible until I made her stop so we could go back and she could rest her legs. She finished the whole book in about 4 days I believe. After she re-stabilized after the surgery, they started turning down the oxygen percentage. This was exciting for us. Every time we went the numbers were lower. 80%, then 60% and lower and lower till we were in the mid 20's. We were ecstatic because that meant she was almost on room air. They started weaning down the amount of morphine she was on and she started to wiggle some. This is where she started developing her new nickname I gave her, squirmy. 4 Days after Mariah's arrival, Maria was well enough to be discharged and we moved back into the Ronald McDonald house.

As the days passed, she was doing great, there were no complications from the surgery, she was doing everything she was supposed to be doing and we began to breathe a little bit. We came in one day and as I walked up to Mariah's room, I could see a bright blue light coming from inside. We walked up and there was a huge UV light above her little bed. I started freaking out wondering what was going on and then was informed that she had developed Jaundice, which isn't uncommon and not really an issue, they just had to supplement some vitamins provided by the light. She got to tan for about 2 days and then all was good. By this point in time, I was running out of vacation time and sick time at work. I hadn't been at work in about 2 weeks. I needed to go back and work until the weekend and then come back. I reluctantly left my family in Houston and came back to work Thursday and Friday, then headed back Friday night. Maria had called me Friday to let me know that Mariah was doing so well, they were going to remove the breathing tubes down her throat and install a breathing mask called a CPAP mask. I was elated. My baby was improving. She also told me that they were going to move her out of the isolated room and into the general population area of the NICU. Another big step for tiny feet. We were on our way.

When I got there Friday night, I was amazed. My baby didn't have big tubes down her throat, she looked somewhat more comfortable. The morphine drip was now not a drip, it was just a dose as needed if the nurses thought she was in pain. She didn't need it much. They were weaning her off of the dopamine to control her blood pressure also. After a day, they also were able to turn off the heater above the bed because she was maintaining a good temperature. More amazing steps. She was getting her nutrition, at this point in time through an IV fluid mixture that had everything she would need, she also had a separate IV of Lipids for the necessary fats she would need.

Right before Mariah's surprise visit, the doctors had briefly talked to us about breast feeding. Maria hadn't done it with either of the other kids, and although she wasn't completely opposed to it, I could tell it wasn't something she was dying to try. The doctors told us that given Mariah's condition, that breast milk would be the best thing possible to aid her in a speedy recovery. No more was needed to be said, Maria was 100% on board. She was mainly concerned that all the medicine she was on would transfer into the baby through the milk, but the nurses assured us that all the meds were breast milk friendly. The day following Mariah's delivery, a breast milk coach came to our room with a bag full of goodies and started teaching us.

Maria has been pumping since day 2. She has been doing amazing and I have learned quite a lot myself. The hospital has a milk bank so while we were admitted, she would pump every 3 hours. The first few days, she would get maybe 20cc's of milk total. They told us that was great for a beginner. As the days progressed the amount increased. She would pump and I would label the bottles and we would go deliver to the milk bank. Once Mariah could start having milk, she would start to grow faster and we wanted that to happen fast. When Mariah was not quite 2 weeks. They started her on milk. They started her out with 7cc's of milk every 3 hours. This wasn't much but we had to watch closely, remember babies with CDH have a tendency to regurgitate food and have problems feeding.

Due to the CPAP mask, she had to be fed with a small tube that was run through her mouth, down into her stomach. The food was fed just by gravity. They would put it in a large syringe and tape it to the side of her bed above her and gravity would just pull the food down into her belly. 2 days passed and no regurgitating happened so they upped the amount to 14cc's. 2 days passed so they upped it to 21cc's. She tolerated that well so they upped it to 28cc's the next day. Then 35, then 40. Now we are at 55cc's of milk every 3 hours with no problems. Maria and I were amazed.

We couldn't believe the fight this little girl had and she was doing so well. The doctors would even make remarks about how well she was doing and they couldn't believe that she was a preemie. I mean she was born a month and 10 days early and weighed more then a lot of full term baby's. Days passed and she was doing great. She was digesting the milk perfectly, they knew because she was quite well at giving the nurses wonderful gifts of full diapers. I was traveling back and forth, working and coming up on the weekends and Maria never left her side. I would have to call and tell her to go back to the RMD house to rest. The nurses started letting her change the diapers. She loved it.

One weekend when I was up, I was there and Maria had stepped out to pump. The nurse asked me if I wanted to change the diaper. Sure I said. It had been 10 years since I changed a diaper; the last diaper I put on was on Celeste. I'm sure it was just like riding a bike, how hard could it be? I started the task and the nurse was guiding me, I don't remember it being this hard. But to be fair to myself, there were lots of wires and things I had to work around. Just my luck, this was not your average run of the mill dirty diaper. I knew at that point that her body was doing what it was supposed to with the milk, maybe too good to be exact. After my eyes re-focused I began wiping, the nurse then stopped me and instructed me that "on little girls you always wipe front to back". I apologized, I don't know why, it wasn't her I was wiping, and began again.

I got it all done and maneuvered the clean diaper into position. I hesitated for a moment, as if I was waiting for the silent approval from the nurse and all of a sudden I heard a noise. There, spread eagle, free as a bird Mariah continued her present for me, apparently she hadn't finished. The nurse said to just let it go and we'd get another diaper. So I waited patiently and when she was done, I cleaned her up, the right way and started over. I got the new diaper on right as another nurse came by to check Mariah's heartbeat, temp and other vitals. As she listened to her heart we both heard a loud noise.

I couldn't believe it. The nurse looked at me and I looked at the other nurse and she had a smirk on her face. I told the nurse to go ahead and finish the exam and I would address the situation in a bit. Once she finished I changed her diaper again. In the span of 20 minutes I had changed 3 diapers. Mariah was helping me catch up to Maria in 1 day. Needless to say, I was a pro after that. But I always let Maria handle it if she wants to.

By this time Mariah was at 21.5% oxygen. Room air or close enough. Maria called me in the middle of the week to inform me that they were going to remove Mariah's CPAP mask and see how she does on her own. I knew she could breathe on her own because when the nurses would give her a bath, they took it off, and they let us bathe her one time, and she had it off for a good 15 minutes. I loved it. I don't like the mask, its big and looks just plain uncomfortable. I know she needs it so I don't make a big deal out of it, but I hate it almost as much as she hates it herself.

When we gave her a bath I was on cloud 9. I could see my baby's beautiful face, she was happy, excited, looking around trying to figure the word out. I can't explain the feeling I got seeing her look around in amazement. I just knew I wanted to feel that for the rest of my life. When the doctors decided to give it a go, they took the mask off in the morning. Maria called me to let me know it was off and she was doing great. She sent me pictures of her holding Mariah with no mask. I was envious. But she should be the one to enjoy that because she has been there since day 1.

I felt horrible that I had to leave to work but what could I do. I needed my job to support us, and I've worked there for almost 11 years and for the most part they had been super understanding but I had to work sometimes. I had used up all my vacation time and sick time with this situation, and I certainly could have stayed gone from work but now, I would be getting docked pay for every day I missed. We needed the money so I left. I just knew that Maria was going to resent me for leaving. I knew she would think that I was back home, having a grand old time, hanging out with my friends and not having a care in the world. I knew she would feel that way, but she didn't.

She knew I was doing what I had to do and she didn't hold it against me. It was hard for us, her being so far away having to be strong for herself, our 10 year old daughter, and the little bundle of joy that had recently arrived. We had some hard days there for a while but we got through it like we always do, and to this day I believe we are stronger than ever now. I have the utmost respect for her, doing what she has done and is currently doing asI write this. She is far stronger than I am. I will be the first to admit that. That's why I love her. The mask being off lasted for about 24 hours. Maria called me the following morning and said they were putting it back on. Mariah had began "de-sating" as they call it during the night and that morning they took x-rays and her lungs weren't expanding as much as they should.

She assured me that the doc's weren't too concerned and the consensus was maybe they jumped the gun a little bit and we would try again in a week. I made it back up there on the weekend and got to see my baby. She had the mask on and I didn't like it but what could I do? I got to hold her and that was the greatest feeling in the world. The nurse told us we could get her a mobile for when she got a crib. The hospital provides medical cribs for the babies once they are well enough to graduate out of the small beds. Maria and I tracked down a Babies r us and found one we liked. Mariah didn't get a crib yet because they were currently out of them so I rigged the mobile up to work on her bed.

The moment I turned it on she was captivated. It had little bugs on it that would light up and it played music. I saw such amazement in those eyes it left me speechless. I felt like I had just done the greatest thing in the world and boy did it feel good. We stayed there till about 1am that night just watching her

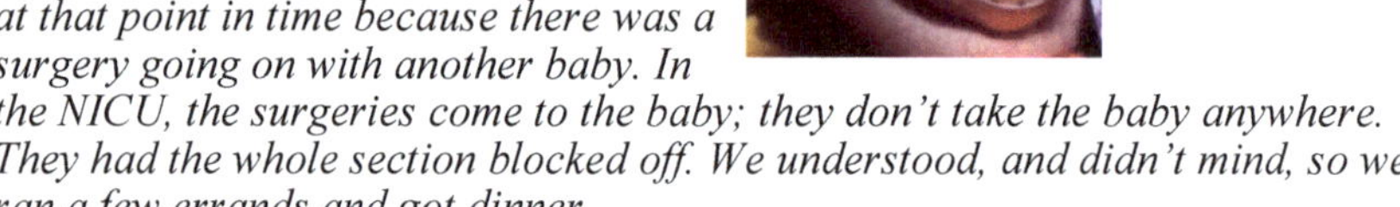

watch the mobile. A few days passed by, I had gone back to San Marcos and Maria called me to tell me that Mariah got her crib. I had to work on Saturday, so I arrived in Houston around 9pm. Maria informed me that we couldn't go see her at that point in time because there was a surgery going on with another baby. In the NICU, the surgeries come to the baby; they don't take the baby anywhere. They had the whole section blocked off. We understood, and didn't mind, so we ran a few errands and got dinner.

The NICU has 24 hour visiting so the nurse assured us we could come whenever the surgery was done. About 10:30pm Maria called and the surgery was still underway so the nurse said she would call us when it was done. At 1:30am we got the call and we went in so I could see my baby. This was the first time I had seen the crib. The mobile was on the crib where it was supposed to be and she had more room to squirm. At this point the nurse told us that we could get her a small swing. Maria and I made a mental note that tomorrow, or later that day actually we would go get her a swing. We stayed about an hour and were getting tired so I made Maria leave with me so we could get some sleep. We got up the next morning and had breakfast and headed to the NICU not knowing we were going to have the day we had. We got to the NICU about 10:00am.

We went to Mariah's section and told her good morning. The nurse asked if I wanted to hold her, and of course I did. We did our dance of lifting and holding wires and maneuvering and I got my baby and settled down into the recliner. I hadn't noticed it at first but after I got settled, I saw a large gathering of people around one of the units with a baby. I thought it odd at first because in the NICU you are only allowed 4 visitors. They enforce it strictly too. I saw *about 8 people, not doctors or nurses around a particular baby. A few minutes later I saw the nurses start bringing in the breast feeding shields to block the area they were in. Maria and I looked at each other kind of putting 2 and 2 together thinking something was wrong.*

We watched people come and go from there and started seeing nurses gather around. At one point I saw a nurse reach up and turn the monitor off that has all the vital stats for the baby. I had a bad feeling. About 2:00 pm I told Maria that we should leave and go get the swing for Mariah. She was excited about getting it so we left Mariah with my mother and father in law and went to find a swing. We got back a little after 3:30 and as we walked through the NICU unit I noticed that where the baby was that all the people were gathered, everything was gone. We got to Mariah and I asked my mother in law if she knew what had happened? She informed us that unfortunately the young baby boy had passed away. She also informed us that the mother was now in the isolated room right behind us, with the doors shut and the blinds pulled, holding her son. It really hit Maria and I hard. We couldn't imagine the pain the lady was feeling, and we both knew deep down that it all too easily could have been us in that situation and it hurt. It hurt badly.

Close to 6pm, I saw the father come out of the room with his son bundled up in a blanket. He handed his son to the nurse and he gathered his wife, and small daughter (5-6yrs) and they walked out of the NICU. My eyes got watery; I didn't know what to do. I silently looked at him, saying in my mind that I was so sorry for his loss. My heart was up in my throat for a few hours and we didn't sleep well that night. I can't imagine the night that family had. Or the days they are still having right now.

I truly feel for them and hope they will be fine. I had to leave at 4am that morning to get to work by 7. I was quiet most of the day; I told a couple of friends what had happened just because they kept asking me what was wrong. It affected me more than I thought and Id never want to have to experience that again and hope I never do. The following week was humbling. I really got a better grasp on what was going on with my baby and how lucky we were. The weekend couldn't come soon enough. Maria called me to inform me that they were going to try and remove the CPAP mask again on Thursday. I wanted to be there for that. Since im only there on weekends, I don't get to talk to the doctors any and they don't make any major changes on weekends either so I don't get to be there for any of that. So I am going to take the hit in my paycheck and take Thursday and Friday off. I'm off that weekend too so it will give me a long weekend with my family and I will get to see how Mariah does this time around with the CPAP off.

<u>Our family becomes whole again</u>

When I came home this time, I was prepping things at home because hopefully we were going to bring Mariah home soon. There was chatter for August 18th. Maria got excited and we were able to breathe. I was back home but I felt relief because Maria was happy that we they would be coming home soon. Monday went as usual, no big changes with Mariah, they had upped her feed amount and she seemed to be doing fine, they were going to do a swallow function test because she had thrown up a couple of times.

Tuesday came around and Maria was getting discouraged. The swallow function test showed that when Mariah drank breast milk, small amounts went into her lungs so they decided that she would drink formula mixed with rice cereal. This really wasn't a big deal but Maria felt it was a step back, they also said they wanted to get her on some medicine because they feel she had acid reflux. Maria felt like these things would postpone them coming home, and also, the NICU physician had stated they wanted to do an Echocardiogram on Mariah on the 21st. This discouraged Maria even more. I knew we were almost there, but I wasn't the one constantly away from home either. I know she was anxious to come home, but we had to make sure everything was ok.

There were a few things we had to do before we could bring Mariah home. I had taken delivery of the oxygen machine and tanks at our home in San Marcos, those had to be there before she could come home, and I was instructed on how to use them. An oxygen tank along with a pulse / oxygen meter was also shipped to the hospital for Maria to be trained on, and Mariah had to be hooked up to them to come home. She got trained in that and we had everything done. I was flying through the week waiting for the weekend so I could go back and see my babies. On Thursday, Maria called me and she sounded upbeat. She said she didn't want to jinx it but the doctors had decided that Mariah should be able to go home on Saturday, the 17th. I couldn't believe it. I was going to get my family home. Friday came around and I left work at 5 and flew to Houston as fast as I could. We began packing things up in the Ronald Mcdonald house and then went to the hospital. The nurse gave us a list of the prescription medicine that we would need to get before Mariah came home. We got the medicine and went back to the hospital to sit with Mariah for a few hours. We left somewhat early that night to get some good rest. We came back Saturday Morning, loaded up our things, filled out all the paperwork and discharged from the hospital. It was a wonderful feeling. We were headed home with our baby. She was going to be home for the first time in her life. She was just shy of 2 months old. Once we got home, we were elated. We couldn't take her anywhere because she is still to fragile. Family came over, but we were very precautious. It was great to be home but we definitely had to adjust. See at the hospital, when we would leave and go sleep, nurses would stay and take care of our baby. Now, we had to feed her every 3 hours, it took some getting used to but we are on a roll now. We have things coming together and I cannot wait to go home every day to see my baby.

A Miracle From A Miracle

Having a baby with Congenital Diaphragmatic Hernia (CDH) raises a lot of questions. The diagnosis often comes as a surprise and leaves parents wondering what else is possible. Since this diagnosis occurs in every 1 in 2,500 live births, we question how we ended up being the parents that beat the odds. A few questions we ask ourselves is if it is possible for us to have another child with this condition if we get pregnant again. We also wonder if our children with CDH can get pregnant, how dangerous it would be if they did, and if their children can have CDH as well. One such mother was Janice Crawford of North Carolina, who gave birth to survivor, Angelia Crawford-Shelton, on January 24th, 1991.

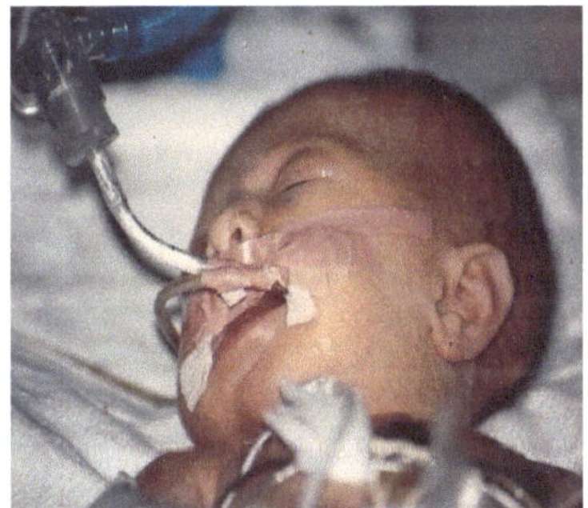

Angelia Crawford-Shelton spent several months in the neonatal intensive care unit and became a NICU graduate in July of 1991. She has also had twelve surgeries, four of which were related to her condition.She is now 27 years old and the mother of a healthy son who was born in November of 2015. Her birth, her survival, and her pregnancy were all miraculous despite this horrible birth defect.

<u>**SpecialCityLife Blog by Marcy Rosamonda**</u>

January 2, 2018

Dear Readers,

It's my first blog of 2018! A lot has happened since I last posted! First of all, I want to say belated happy holidays!

My son got a Bronchoscopy done the Thursday before Christmas to find out what is going on with his trachea because a CT scan after Thanksgiving showed it had shifted and we were hoping that's all it was. The Bronchoscopy showed that it has started to twist. It was at 90 degrees when they did the Bronchoscopy and the upper-lobe of his left lung has been almost blocked off. What this means is if anything goes into that part of his lung he will not be able to cough it up and so he is at high risk for pneumonia right now. We find out the plan to fix this tomorrow so needless to say I'm a nervous wreck!

We had a quiet Christmas because we have to be really careful where we go right now. So, we went to my in laws because my husbands brother flew in from Seattle, but everyone that came had not been sick in the past week and there were no other kids. Unfortunately we weren't able to go to my sisters for Christmas because she has a son that is around my sons age so it was too risky. I really wish that we could have gone but it was just too risky so my mom came over for a visit later that week and we watched shows on Netflix and talked.

I didn't really do much for New Years because my son has been waking up at 2:30 a.m. each morning for the past couple weeks so I've been very tired! On the plus side my son is almost walking and babbles a lot more than he used to! He actually tells you off now it's hilarious!

He did get his back brace. However we are getting it evaluated by his Dr tomorrow. It really limits him and rubs on his G-tube, so we may have to get a different brace. I hate how much it limits him–he can't even sit in it. He is now eating half a container of baby food each morning! We have also been giving him finger foods like a bread stick, some biscuits and the occasional French fry or potato chip just to get him to eat more and it's helping!

Thank you for reading!

While a few survivors can live fairly normal lives, others end up with a variety of medical issues. Survivors can face years of speech therapy, physical therapy, medicines, oxygen and feeding tubes that they have to rely on to live, and medications. One such survivor is Robbie Trejo:

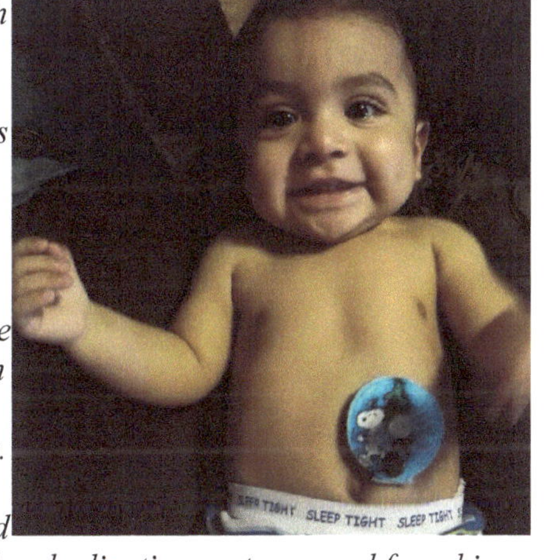

Robbie was diagnosed in utero with left Congenital Diaphragmatic Hernia. He was born on February 20, 2017. He weighed 8 lbs and was 19 inches long. We found out that Robbie had no left diaphragm. He went into emergency surgery at 4 days old. He spent 32 days on life support and I got to hold him for the first time at 34 days old. He was on the Oscillator, Conventional Ventilator, and off the wall Oxygen. He had his gtube placed on May 4th. He reherniated on May 6th and had to have his gtube replaced, a duplication cyst removed from his stomach, and a Nissen Fundoplication during his second repair surgery. Robbie spent 92 days in Cook Children's NICU in Fort Worth, TX. About a week prior to discharge we found out Robbie suffered a brain injury while on life support. Robbie was discharged from the NICU on May 22, 2017. He

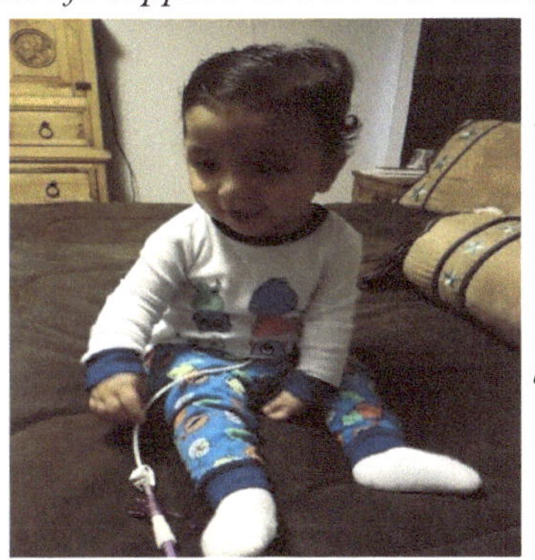

does Feeding Therapy, Occupational Therapy, and Physical Therapy twice weekly. He is exclusively gtube fed. He has since then been diagnosed with Asthma, Pulmonary Hypertension, Pulmonary Hypoplasia, Chronic Lung Disease, and Plagiocephaly. He spent 9 weeks in a doc band to help correct the Plagiocephaly. He came home on Ativan, Gabapentin, Methadone, Clonidine Patch, Nexium, Pulmicort, and Albuterol. We successfully weaned him off the Methadone, Ativan, Clonidine, and Gabapentin. He is followed by his Dietician, Gasteroenterology, Cardiology, Neurology, Pulmonology, NEST Clinic, Neonatology, and his Pediatrician. Robbie has made great strides to get to where he is today! Motor skill wise he is at about a 6 month level which is HUGE for him. We are so proud of our miracle boy!

-Tanya Trejo

<u>List of Hospitals</u>

List of Hospitals that offer hope for CDH Babies:

<u>Arkansas</u>

Arkansas Children's Hospital

<u>California</u>

University San Francisco Fetal Treatment Center, CHOPs (UCSF)

Huntington Memorial Hospital (Pasadena, California)

University of California San Francisco Benioff Children's Hospital

Harbor General UCLA

Ronald Reagan UCLA Medical Center/Fetal Center

<u>Colorado</u>

Children's Hospital of Colorado

<u>Florida</u>

John Hopkin's All Children's Hospital

<u>Georgia</u>

Children's Healthcare of Atlanta (Egleston)

<u>Illinois</u>

Lurie's Children's Hospital in Chicago

Ochsner Baptist Hospital (New Orleans, Louisiana)

<u>Maryland</u>

John Hopkins Hospital (Baltimore)

Michigan

University of Michigan CS Mott Children's Hospital:

Minnesota

Minneapolis Children's Hospital

Missouri

Children's Mercy Hospital (Kansas City)

Cardinal Glennon St. Louis Fetal Care institute

New Mexico

University of New Mexico children's hospital

Ohio

Nationwide Children's Hospital (Columbus, Ohio)

Fetal Care Center/Cincinnati Childrens Hospital (Cincinnati, Ohio)

Cincinnati Children's Hospital:

Oregon

Randal's Children Hospital (Portland, Oregon)

Pennsylvania

Children's Hospital of Philadephia (CHOP)

South Carolina

MUSC Children's Hospital

Tennessee

Monroe Carell Jr. Vanderbilt Children's Hospital (Nashville, TN)

Texas

Cook Children's Hospital (Fort Worth, Texas)

Children's Memorial Hermann Hospital (Houston, Tx)

VCU Children's Hospital (Richmond, Virginia)

Washington

Providence Sacred Heart Children's Hospital (Spokane, WA)

Seattle University of Washington Children's Hospital

International:

Canada

The Hospital For Sick Children

1. Ashley Chatwin's CDH Star, Lucas Chatwin, is scheduled to have G-Tube surgery on February 1st, 2018. Please pray that he has a successful operation and a speedy recovery!

<u>CDH Facts:</u>

1. Only fifty percent of babies diagnosed with congenital diaphragmatic hernia survive.

2. It is possible to have multiple people in one family that are diagnosed with congenital diaphragmatic hernia.

3. It is also possible that older people can be diagnosed with it, not just babies.

4. Congenital diaphragmatic hernia has been found in the animal kingdom before.

5. While it is considered "rare" by definition, it is as common as Bona Spifida but there is less funding and knowledge of it.

6. Some survivors are able to live fairly normal lives after repair surgery. However, there is always a possibility for reherniation: an issue in which the hole in the diaphragm opens back up, allowing for abdominal organs to float back into the chest cavity.

7. Survivors of CDH often have problems feeding. Several survivors are diagnosed as "failure to thrive" - he/she fails to gain weight for their age. Problems gaining weight is a common issue among survivors.

8. Most CDH survivors are not allowed to play contact sports for fear of impact of a ball or colliding with another person, which may cause the hole in the diaphragm to open back up.

ACKNOWLEDGMENTS: ALL OF THE WONDERFUL PEOPLE THAT ALLOWED THIS

1. Ashley Chatwin
2. Janice Crawford
3. Sharon Deaver Weir
4. Bobby Evans
5. Tanya Trejo
6. Kimberly Atkinson
7. Marcy Rosamonda

www.ingramcontent.com/pod-product-compliance
Lightning Source LLC
Chambersburg PA
CBHW040252240726
48664CB00001B/359